Habits of Grace

Enjoying Jesus through
the Spiritual Disciplines
Study Guide

David Mathis

 **CROSSWAY**®

WHEATON, ILLINOIS

Habits of Grace: Enjoying Jesus through the Spiritual Disciplines Study Guide

Copyright © 2016 by David C. Mathis

Published by Crossway
   1300 Crescent Street
   Wheaton, Illinois 60187

Cover design: Jeff Miller, Faceout Studio

Cover image: Benjamin Devine

First printing 2016

Printed in the United States of America

Scripture quotations are from the ESV® Bible (The Holy Bible, English Standard Version®), copyright © 2001 by Crossway, a publishing ministry of Good News Publishers. Used by permission. All rights reserved.

Trade paperback ISBN: 978-1-4335-5353-0
ePub ISBN: 978-1-4335-5356-1
PDF ISBN: 978-1-4335-5354-7
Mobipocket ISBN: 978-1-4335-5355-4

Library of Congress Cataloging-in-Publication Data
Mathis, David, 1980–
 Habits of grace : enjoying Jesus through the spiritual
disciplines / David Mathis ; foreword by John Piper.
  pages cm
 Includes bibliographical references and index.
 ISBN 978-1-4335-5047-8 (tp)
 1. Spiritual life—Christianity. 2. Christian life. I. Title.
BV4501.3.M284   2016
248.4'6—dc23   2015023865

Crossway is a publishing ministry of Good News Publishers.

VP 26 25 24 23 22 21 20 19 18 17 16
15 14 13 12 11 10 9 8 7 6 5 4 3 2 1

Contents

Part 3
BELONG TO HIS BODY (FELLOWSHIP)

Part 4
CODA

How to Use This Study Guide

I have designed this study guide to supplement individual and group studies of *Habits of Grace: Enjoying Jesus through the Spiritual Disciplines* (Crossway, 2016). This workbook draws from and leans on the book such that it makes access to the book essential in understanding and benefitting from this study.

In this study guide, I have parceled out the book's introduction and eighteen chapters into thirty-one sections (or "days"). The hope is to make each section doable in one sitting and to make the whole study doable in one month (thirty-one days), if doing one section each day.

However, it is not my expectation that every participant, or even most, will undertake to complete this study in one focused month. Some may take a section every other day, or multiple in one day, or even only a day or two per week. My hope is that you'll be able to move at your pace, depending on how new or familiar the material is to you, whether you are studying in a group setting or with friends, or whatever life circumstances in which you find yourself.

Each day includes at least one brief passage of Scripture for your reading and meditation as well as one defined section to read from the book *Habits of Grace* before answering the questions. The questions are designed to rehearse and deepen your understanding of the most important information in the chapters, as well as to engage your heart and inner person, and also inspire practical direction and life change.

My prayer for you is that God would richly bless your mind, heart, and daily life as you undertake this study and seek to engage more deeply with the principles and counsel of *Habits of Grace*. And I hope this study proves valuable for years to come. The principles and practices of God's "means of grace" are not flashy or dramatic, but it is often fresh attention to the ordinary that is most life transforming and produces the greatest fruit in the long run.

I am indebted to Pam Eason for her remarkable work in carefully reviewing the first draft of this study guide and bringing her acumen in instructional design to bear on it. The study has been vastly improved by her skill and ingenuity, especially for visual learners. For the more right-brained among us, you have Pam to thank for the many creative ways to enrich the learning process by drawing pictures and finding fresh avenues for synthesizing the material into your own thoughts and applications.

If you plan to read the book's foreword and preface, now would be a good time. When you turn the page to Day 1, we begin with the introduction.

Day 1

Grace Gone Wild

God, being rich in _mercy_, because of the great love with which he loved us, even when we were dead in our trespasses, made us alive together with Christ—by grace you have been saved—and raised us up with him and seated us with him in the heavenly places in Christ Jesus, so that in the coming ages he might show the immeasurable riches of his grace in kindness toward us in Christ Jesus.

Ephesians 2:4–7

Read from the beginning of the introduction through the section "Where the Grace Keeps Passing" (pp. 21–26).

1. Refer to the section "Invading Our Space." Name at least two ways grace has invaded humanity's space.

2. You cannot control or manipulate the grace of God through your various habits and actions. A terrible way to misunderstand this study would be to think that somehow you can. Review the sections "Put Yourself in the Path of God's Grace" and "Where the Grace Keeps Passing." Draw two circles. Title one circle "My Actions and Efforts." Title the other circle "God's Grace." Use symbols or lines, or whatever you would like, to show the relationship between the two circles.

3. Review the section "Flooding the Future." God's grace stretches back into eternity past and forward into eternity future. Ponder that and complete the following:

a) State a surprising fact that you learned from this section about God's grace.

b) Draw a timeline and title it "God's Grace in My Life." Add and label points on the line to represent the stages of life you have passed through up to now (infancy, childhood, adolescence, young adult, etc.). Add notes to the timeline that identify the ways God's grace came to you at these different points in your life, the way God's grace came to you before the timeline began, and the way God's grace will continue after it ends.

4. Ponder the grace that God showed you before you were even able to recognize it. Describe or illustrate with a graph or drawing (1) God's grace that was yours before you were ever born; and (2) God's grace that was already at work even before you first believed.

5. Review the section "Where the Grace Keeps Passing." Explain or illustrate what it means to "position" yourself "to go on getting as [God] keeps on giving."

6. Reflect on your reasons for choosing this study. Complete the following:

   a) My goals for this study are . . .

   b) As a result of this study, I hope . . .

   c) My prayer for this study is . . .

Day 2

The End of the Means

Work out your own salvation with fear and trembling, for it is God who works in you, both to will and to work for his good pleasure.

Philippians 2:12–13

Read the section "What Means of Grace Means and Doesn't" through the end of the introduction (pp. 26–33).

1. Review the section "What Means of Grace Means and Doesn't." Name the one who supplies your "exertions of effort" toward Christlikeness.

2. Carefully read Romans 15:18; 1 Corinthians 15:10; Philippians 2:12–13; Colossians 1:29; Hebrews 13:20–21; and 1 Peter 4:11. Explain or illustrate with a drawing the dynamic of God working in you through your effort and actions.

3. Once again refer to the section "What Means of Grace Means and Doesn't." If you are a Christian, you experience both justification and sanctification. Explain or illustrate:

a) the function of grace in justification

b) the function of grace in sanctification

c) the difference between justification and sanctification

4. In the section "How to Receive the Gift of Effort," I said that the way to receive the gift of God's empowering our actions is to do the actions. If he gives the gift of effort, we receive that gift *by* expending the effort. When he gives the grace of growing in holiness, we don't receive that gift apart from becoming more holy. When he gives us the desire to get more of him in the Scriptures, or in prayer, or among his people, we don't receive that gift without experiencing the desire and living out the pursuits that flow from it. Essential to thriving in the means of grace is taking ownership of the reality, deep in your soul, that God's grace comes to you not only despite your effort (justification), but also in your effort (sanctification). His grace is never earned by your works, but it does work in you to produce holy desires and actions. Imagine that you are talking to a friend. Write an explanation or draw an illustration of this truth in a way that your friend could understand.

5. In the section "Lay Yourself in the Way of Allurement," I quoted Jonathan Edwards, who said that you can "endeavor to promote spiritual appetites by *laying yourself in the way of allurement*." Identify the one who attracts or allures and the one who needs to be attracted or allured.

6. Read Luke 18:35–43 and 19:1–10. Both Bartimaeus and Zacchaeus put themselves in Jesus's path. Summarize or illustrate what their stories teach about receiving God's grace.

7. Review the section "The Great End of the Means." Describe or illustrate "the great end" of the means of grace.

8. Read Philippians 3:7–8; John 17:3; and Hosea 6:3. Most likely, you want to cultivate habits of grace in your own life because you are aiming for one or more specific goals. Write your goal(s) below.

9. Once again, refer back to the section "The Great End of the Means." Answer the following questions:

    a) Why is it inadequate, or at least not ultimate, to say that the goal of Christian disciplines is spiritual growth, or godliness, or holiness?

    b) What danger do you face if your focus becomes your own transformation rather than knowing and enjoying Jesus?

10. In the section "The Means of Grace and the Things of Earth," I explained that this study focuses on what we might call the *special* means of God's grace, as in the *special* revelation of his word, prayer, and his redeemed body. But God also is pleased to work for our spiritual good and benefit through *general* means of his grace—as in nature, food, sleep, exercise, music, and more. Describe or illustrate a recent experience in which one of God's general means had a tangible effect on your soul.

11. Likely you've heard of the spiritual disciplines in the past and tried them yourself in some way, shape, or form. Review the last two paragraphs of the introduction. Summarize or illustrate how you expect this study to be different.

Part 1

HEAR HIS VOICE

Word

Day 3

Shape Your Life with the Words of Life

Do all things without grumbling or disputing, that you may be blameless and innocent, children of God without blemish in the midst of a crooked and twisted generation, among whom you shine as lights in the world, holding fast to the word of life, so that in the day of Christ I may be proud that I did not run in vain or labor in vain.

Philippians 2:14–16

Read chapter 1 through the section "The Word Pervasive" (pp. 37–41).

1. In the section "The Word Original," I quoted John Frame, who said that God's word is "his powerful, authoritative self-expression." List three ways God has revealed himself to you through his word.

2. Often we identify God's word with the Bible. This can be a good thing since the Bible is indeed God's word written. However, this limited category restricts your understanding of "God's word." Explain or use a drawing to illustrate how the categories "the Word incarnate" and "the word evangelical" enrich your understanding of God's word.

3. Refer to your answer to number 2 above. Explain or illustrate what practical effects your understanding of these categories will have on your efforts to immerse yourself in God's word.

4. Refer to the section "The Word Pervasive." Explain:

a) why God's voice is the most fundamental principle of the means of grace.

b) why God's word has a kind of primacy over prayer (having God's ear) and fellowship (belonging to Christ's body, the church).

5. Consider the various categories of God's word. First and foremost contemplate Jesus, God's Word. Next, reflect on the gospel, God's message to humanity. Finally, consider the Scriptures, God's inspired, inerrant written word. Answer the following questions:

a) Do your thoughts about these categories motivate you to create practices that will shape your life with the entire range of God's word?

b) If so, what specific practices come to mind?

c) Which practices, of those that came to your mind, seem most life giving?

d) Do you foresee turning these life-giving practices into lifestyle habits? Why or why not?

6. In the section "The Word Written," I encouraged you to fashion rhythms of life that help you revolve around having God's incarnate Word, by God's gospel word, through God's written word. In light of the practices that came to mind in number 5 above, and before moving on to the specific ideas and suggestions that lie ahead in this book, take a few moments now to think about how these habits might fit into your current season of life. What regular rhythms and specific practices of life—daily, weekly, monthly, or however regular—do you see yourself using to engage yourself with God's word?

_____

"No Spiritual Discipline is more important than the intake of God's Word. Nothing can substitute for it. There simply is no healthy Christian life apart from a diet of the milk and meat of Scripture."—Donald S. Whitney

_____

Day 4

Preaching the Gospel to Yourself

Now I commend you to God and to the word of his grace, which is able to build you up and to give you the inheritance among all those who are sanctified.

Acts 20:32

Read "More on Preaching to Yourself" to the end of chapter 1 (pp. 41–42). Use words or drawings to answer the following questions.

1. What does it mean to "preach the gospel to yourself"?

2. How is preaching the gospel to yourself distinct from Bible reading?

3. How is regular Bible reading essential to preaching the gospel to yourself?

4. What captures your idle thoughts? What fears or hopes fill your spare moments?

5. Reflect on your answer to number 4 above. How would you preach the gospel to yourself in view of your specific need? Write a short gospel sermon to yourself below.

6. Martyn Lloyd-Jones wrote, "Have you realized that most of your unhappiness in life is due to the fact that you are listening to yourself instead of talking to yourself? Take those thoughts that come to you the moment you wake up in the morning. You have not originated them, but they start talking to you, they bring back the problems of yesterday, etc. Somebody is talking . . . yourself is talking to you!"[1]

a. Perhaps you identify with what it's like to "listen to yourself." Consider how easily and often this happens. Describe your experience of "listening to yourself."

b. How should you talk to yourself when you recognize that you are listening to a voice that is not God's?

"Hearing the word of the cross, and preaching it to ourselves, is the central strategy for sinners in the fight for joy."—John Piper

----

[1] D. Martyn Lloyd-Jones, *Spiritual Depression: Its Causes and Cure* (Grand Rapids, MI: Eerdmans, 1965), 20.

Bible Reading Is an Art

[Jesus] said to them, "O foolish ones, and slow of heart to believe all that the prophets have spoken! Was it not necessary that the Christ should suffer these things and enter into his glory?" And beginning with Moses and all the Prophets, he interpreted to them in all the Scriptures the things concerning himself.

Luke 24:25–27

Whatever was written in former days was written for our instruction, that through endurance and through the encouragement of the Scriptures we might have hope.

Romans 15:4

Read from the beginning of chapter 2 through the section "The Whole Thing?" (pp. 43–49).

1. Circle the best way to learn the art of reading the Bible.

a) Know the fundamentals of language and communication.

b) Read about reading.

c) Refer to commentaries.

d) Attend classes on inductive Bible study.

e) Read the Bible for yourself.

2. Refer to the sections "Learn the Art through Practice" and "Discover the Art of Meditation." Complete the following sentences:

a) Bible reading is . . .

b) Bible study is . . .

c) Bible meditation is . . .

3. Jesus's apostles learned to see him throughout the Scriptures. This doesn't mean that they artificially imported him into every detail of the text. Instead, they learned to see how all the Scriptures anticipated his person and work. They saw how Scripture authentically pointed to the centrality of his life and mission in God's plan for rescuing humanity from our sin. Describe or illustrate how you will avoid the two Bible-reading extremes of (1) missing Jesus where he is, and (2) seeing him where he isn't.

4. Perhaps you have read the whole Bible through. If so, summarize your experience and the value of it. If not, explain or illustrate what holds you back.

5. Donald S. Whitney says, "The basic difference between Bible reading and Bible study is simply a pen and paper (or some other means of preserving your thoughts)."[2] Explain what you think he means.

---

[2] Donald S. Whitney, *Spiritual Disciplines for the Christian Life*, rev. ed. (Colorado Springs: NavPress, 2014), 32.

Day 6

The X Factor in Bible Reading

When the Spirit of truth comes, he will guide you into all the truth, for he will not speak on his own authority, but whatever he hears he will speak, and he will declare to you the things that are to come. He will glorify me, for he will take what is mine and declare it to you.

John 16:13–14

In chapter 2 read the section "More Than Just Raking" through the end of the chapter (pp. 49–54).

1. Circle the phrase that best describes you.

When I study the Bible, I

    a) make notes with pen and paper.

    b) make notes on my computer.

    c) keep reading. I do not like to stop reading long enough to make notes or write questions.

2. In the section "Digging in Divine Words," I said that some Christians naturally incline to a slower gear, and they need the reminder to press forward for breadth, keep the larger context in view, and reflect on the big picture, not just individual verses. But others of us tend toward raking.

a) Draw a stick figure to represent yourself. Add either a rake or a shovel to your hand.

b) Explain or illustrate how you will compensate for your natural inclination to either rake or dig.

3. Circle the statements that best describe your specific Bible reading and studying needs.

a) I need to read for breadth to get a better sense of the whole story of Jesus's rescue for sinners.

b) I need to read for breadth to get a sense of the structure and shape of Scripture.

c) I need to pause more regularly to ask hard questions about what I'm reading.

d) I need to pause more regularly to propose answers to hard questions I have.

4. In the section "The X Factor in Bible Reading," I described in a variety of ways the relationship between the Spirit and God's word.

a) Circle the description(s) below that best helped you understand this relationship.

- A strange, enigmatic power stirs when you reach for the Scriptures.

- An influential, invisible movement happens when you encounter God's word.

- A personal, divine, mysterious, indomitable, and irresistible force makes the seemingly simple act of reading and studying God's word into something supernatural.

- The Spirit strengthens the soul in obvious and subtle ways as you encounter God's word.

b) Perhaps there are other descriptions in this section that added to your understanding. If so, write them here.

5. The Bible is a big book. Its message and major teachings are simple and clear, but it has many difficult sections and teachings that can be hard to follow. Refer back to number 4 above. Explain the effect these truths, related to the Spirit as your helper, have on

a) your soul.

b) the way you approach the Bible.

Day 7

Warm Yourself at the Fire of Meditation

Let the word of Christ dwell in you richly, teaching and admonishing one another in all wisdom, singing psalms and hymns and spiritual songs, with thankfulness in your hearts to God.

Colossians 3:16

Read chapter 3 (pp. 55–60).

1. Refer to the section "Meditation Made Christian."

a) Define Christian meditation.

b) Explain or illustrate how Christian meditation is distinct from "meditation" in other worldviews.

2. In the section "Meditation Day and Night," I speculated about why I think meditation is a lost art today. Consider your life and the lives of those you know best. Complete the following statement: I think meditation is a lost art because . . .

3. Refer to the section "Meditation Is the Missing Link." Explain in your own words, or illustrate with a drawing, what it means that meditation is "the missing link" between hearing God's voice in his word and having his ear in prayer.

4. Refer again to the section "Meditation Is the Missing Link." Explain or illustrate how

a) Bible study differs from meditation.

b) Bible study is connected to meditation.

5. In the section "The High Point of Daily Devotions," I said that I think of meditation as the high point of my daily devotional time. Explain why everyone should say the same.

6. Thomas Watson, the English Puritan author and pastor, said, "The reason we come away so cold from reading the word is, because we do not warm ourselves at the fire of meditation." Consider your own recent attempts at Bible reading without meditation, then answer the following questions.

a) Did you come away cold?

b) What was your heart truly looking for in God's word?

c) What was needed to warm your heart?

7. Consider your regular habits of hearing God's voice in the Scriptures. List ways to make meditation a consistent high point.

Bring the Bible Home to Your Heart

Be doers of the word, and not hearers only, deceiving yourselves. For if anyone is a hearer of the word and not a doer, he is like a man who looks intently at his natural face in a mirror. For he looks at himself and goes away and at once forgets what he was like. But the one who looks into the perfect law, the law of liberty, and perseveres, being no hearer who forgets but a doer who acts, he will be blessed in his doing.

James 1:22–25

Read chapter 4 (pp. 61–65).

1. "Take every word as spoken to yourselves." Evaluate your Bible reading in light of this quote from Thomas Watson, found in the section "God's Word Is for You."

a) Circle the statement that best describes your evaluation.

- I am inclined to read the Bible in a very personal way.

- I naturally distance myself from the corrections, examples, instructions, and encouragements I find in Scripture.

b) List truths you need to keep in mind to balance out your Bible reading, study, and meditation proclivities.

2. Reread 2 Timothy 3:16–17; 1 Corinthians 10:6, 11; and Romans 15:4 in the section "God's Word Is for You." Draw a sticky note below. Add a clear, short, and

memorable reminder to yourself to convey the messages that (1) the Bible really is for you, and (2) Scripture really is for daily application to your mind, heart, and life.

3. The nature of the Christian life is not becoming a better and better list-keeper. Rather, the nature of the Christian life is increasingly becoming a kind of person who is able to discern God's will in complicated and unique circumstances. Review the section "Specific Applications for Every Day?" and notice how Paul prays in Romans 12:2; Philippians 1:9–10; and Colossians 1:9–10. Add your own comments to further clarify the nature of the Christian life.

4. In the section "Specific Applications for Every Day?" I said that true and lasting change happens in a less straightforward way than we may be prone to think. Explain or illustrate:

   a) the "less straightforward way" to true and lasting change.

b) how this "less straightforward way" to true and lasting change makes you think differently about biblical application.

5. In the section "God's Word Is for Seeing," I discussed the most important kind of "application" that should be pursued when you encounter God's word. Describe or illustrate that application.

6. In the section "God's Word Is for Seeing," I quoted John Piper, who said, "We go to the Bible to be astonished, to be amazed at God and Christ and the cross and grace and the gospel." I followed up by noting that this astonishment is the most important scriptural application to pursue and that it is really just another way of commending meditation. Explain or illustrate how commending the pursuit of astonishment is the same as commending meditation.

7. Some people come to the Bible looking for things to do. Others come to the Bible to see and feel. Describe or illustrate the results of each approach.

8. Circle the aspect of application that should be your priority.

- application to your heart and inner life.

- application to your outer life.

9. Perhaps you have read a passage of Scripture and tried to apply it to your outer life. Describe the long-term results.

10. Perhaps, when you read Scripture, you generally apply it to your inner life. Describe the long-term results.

———————————————

"Seek to understand first how God's words fell on the original hearers, and how they relate to Jesus's person and work, and then bring them home to yourself."—Habits of Grace, p. 62

———————————————

Day 9

Memorize the Mind of God

The natural person does not accept the things of the Spirit of God, for they are folly to him, and he is not able to understand them because they are spiritually discerned. The spiritual person judges all things, but is himself to be judged by no one. "For who has understood the mind of the Lord so as to instruct him?" But we have the mind of Christ.

                                    1 Corinthians 2:14–16

Read chapter 5 through section "Two Great Effects" (pp. 67–72).

1. The introductory paragraphs in chapter 5 advocate a "change in perspective" when it comes to Scripture memorization. Refer to the section "Mold Your Mind for Today." Describe or illustrate this change in perspective.

2. Refer to the sections "Some Call It 'Meditation'"; "Reset Your Mind on the Things of the Spirit"; and "The Mind of Christ Is Yours." List ways meditation and Scripture memorization work together.

3. Complete the statement(s) that best fits you.

- I have never tried to memorize Scripture because . . . (Be sure to dig beneath the excuses of a bad memory or not enough time.)

- I have memorized Scripture in the past, and some techniques I've found helpful are . . .

- I no longer try to memorize Scripture because . . .

- I am currently memorizing Scripture because . . .

"One of the most underrated benefits of memorizing Scripture is that it provides fuel for meditation." –Donald S. Whitney

---

Five Tips for Bible Memory

Let the word of Christ dwell in you richly, teaching and admonishing one another in all wisdom, singing psalms and hymns and spiritual songs, with thankfulness in your hearts to God.

Colossians 3:16

Read "Five Tips for Bible Memory" through the verse lists (pp. 72–81).

1. List one or two of the five tips for Bible memory you think will be, or have found to be, most helpful.

2. Draw a vertical line below. Add your own Bible memory tip(s) on the left side of the line. Recall any pitfalls you have encountered. Add those pitfalls to the right side of the line.

3. Describe or illustrate a time when some memorized Scripture became a practical help to you in some difficult conversation or temptation to sin.

4. Circle and complete the statement that best describes you:

a) I sometimes turn Scripture memorization into an achievement. The result is that I become prideful and begin to compare myself to others. I need to remind myself that . . .

b) I tend to avoid Scripture memorization. I reason that it could lead to pride, or I use some other excuse. I need to remind myself that . . .

5. Reread the section under "Take It with You during the Day." Then look carefully through the two lists of gospel verses and passages. Pick two or three you don't know by heart. Develop a plan, in the space below, for learning them.

6. Add your own gospel verse or passage suggestions to this list.

Day 11

Lifelong Learning

[Jesus] said to them, "These are my words that I spoke to you while I was still with you, that everything written about me in the Law of Moses and the Prophets and the Psalms must be fulfilled." Then he opened their minds to understand the Scriptures.

Luke 24:44–45

Read chapter 6 (pp. 83–89).

1. In the introductory paragraphs of chapter 6, I discussed the centrality of teaching in Jesus's ministry as well as in the ongoing ministry of the church. Choose and complete the statement that best describes your reaction to the discussion about the centrality of teaching in Christianity.

a) I think it is odd that ongoing teaching is so important to the Christian faith because . . .

b) I agree that ongoing teaching is very important to the Christian faith because . . .

2. "The focal point and center of our lifelong learning is the person and work of Christ." Circle the statement that best describes your reaction to this statement, and explain more below.

a) It is manifestly true.

b) It is too simplistic.

3. Choose the underlined words that best describe how you feel when you hear that ongoing health in the Christian life is inextricably linked to ongoing learning. Complete the statements.

a) I feel <u>afraid</u>/<u>excited</u> because . . .

b) My <u>fear</u>/<u>excitement</u> may result in pitfalls such as . . .

4. You may be surprised to know how much ongoing learning is already happening in your life and the variety of it. Draw three columns below. In the left column, list the kinds of ongoing learning that you are already involved in. In the middle column, note the context in which this learning takes place (formal classroom learning, on-the-job learning, personal interest learning, one-on-one, etc.), and in the remaining

column, list the type of media that delivers the learning (traditional teachers, podcasts, books, online classes or articles, personal conversation, etc.).

5. Review your current schedule and patterns. Identify times that could be redeemed for learning in your regular rhythm and flow of life. Identify mindless moments that could be taken captive for growth. Describe or illustrate what you discovered.

6. Review your use of social media in light of lifelong learning. Identify who or what fills your feed. Identify the amount of mindless entertainment that distracts you. List steps you could make to take advantage of new and different kinds of media for the purposes of lifelong learning and your advancement in the faith.

7. Add your own principles to the list of "Five Principles for Lifelong Learning." Include the methods and strategies you have found most helpful as you have pursued learning outside the formal classroom.

"God designed the church to be a community of lifelong learners under the earthly guidance of leaders who are teachers at heart."—Habits of Grace, p. 84

Part 2

HAVE HIS EAR

Prayer

Day 12

Enjoy the Gift of Having God's Ear

He is able to save to the uttermost those who draw near to God through him, since he always lives to make intercession for them.

Hebrews 7:25

Read chapter 7 (pp. 93–97).

1. Refer to the section "A Conversation We Didn't Start."

a) Answer the following:

- What is prayer?

- How is prayer like a conversation between two friends?

- How is prayer unlike a conversation between two friends?

b) Explain:

- what it means that "prayer is a conversation we didn't start."

- some things you learned from this section about the nature of prayer.

c) Draw a microphone and an ear. Label the microphone "God's voice." Label the ear "God's Ear." Add lines, symbols, and/or words to illustrate the relationship between "hearing God's voice" and "having his ear."

2. In the section "The Great Purpose of Prayer," I said that prayer is not finally about getting things from God, but getting God.

a) Explain why "getting God" is "the great purpose of prayer."

b) Circle the underlined phrase that best describes your prayer life: My prayers mostly consist of <u>asking for things</u> / <u>confession and repentance</u> / <u>talking with God, adoring God, and enjoying the presence of God.</u>

3. In the section "In Jesus's Name We Pray," I said that our having God's ear is as sure as our having God's Son. Explain what that means.

4. There may have been times when you found praying difficult—perhaps that is true of you even now. Reflect on your prayerless times. List:

a) the internal "heart" reasons that keep you from prayer.

b) the lies you believe when you don't pray.

c) the truths you ignore when you don't pray.

5. Circle the underlined phrase that best describes your satisfaction with your current prayer life: <u>I am totally satisfied</u> / <u>mostly satisfied</u> / <u>somewhat satisfied</u> / <u>not satisfied</u> with my prayer life.

6. Draw two columns. Title the left column "Ways My Prayer Life Is Lacking." Title the right column "Strengths to Build On." Add your own "lacks" and "strengths" to the appropriate columns.

7. Consider your current prayer life, both that which is private and that with fellow Christians. Describe or illustrate:

- evidences of God's grace.

- improvements you would like to make in your private and public prayer life.

Day 13

Pray in Secret

When you pray, you must not be like the hypocrites. For they love to stand and pray in the synagogues and at the street corners, that they may be seen by others. Truly, I say to you, they have received their reward. But when you pray, go into your room and shut the door and pray to your Father who is in secret. And your Father who sees in secret will reward you.

Matthew 6:5–6

Read chapter 8 through the section "Context for Relationship" (pp. 99–102).

1. In the introductory paragraphs of chapter 8, I quoted Francis Chan, who said that his "biggest concern for this generation is your inability to focus, especially in prayer." Decide if you agree, then revise and complete each statement below to make them true:

a) I have friends who find it difficult to sustain focus, especially in prayer, because . . .

b) I struggle to sustain focus, especially in prayer, because . . .

2. Refer to the section "Praying 'in the Closet.'" Explain why "closet prayer" (private prayer) is so important.

3. Refer to the section "Context for Relationship." Illustrate or explain:

a) what it means that private prayer is "a context for relationship";

b) your thoughts about private prayer;

c) why, as J. I. Packer writes, how we pray "is as important a question as we can ever face";

d) the difference it might make in your life to think about prayer as "a context for relationship."

4. Carefully review the Scripture texts in the section "Context for Relationship." List your observations about the prayer life of Jesus. Place an asterisk (*) beside the observations that may prove helpful in building and shaping your own prayer life.

"[How we pray] is as important a question as we can ever face."—J. I. Packer

---

Day 14

The Power and Privilege of Private Prayer

We have a great high priest who has passed through the heavens, Jesus, the Son of God. . . . Let us then with confidence draw near to the throne of grace, that we may receive mercy and find grace to help in time of need.

Hebrews 4:14–16

In chapter 8 read "Five Suggestions for Secret Prayer" through the end of the chapter (pp. 103–6).

1. Describe or draw your current or possible go-to spot for regular private prayer.

2. List some steps you can take to keep your prayer habits fresh.

3. List one or two new habits you want to cultivate to enrich your private prayer time—or, if your private prayer time needs a full overhaul, write a new Private Prayer Plan.

4. Consider the content of your private prayers in view of ACTS. Circle the statement below that best describes your prayers:

a) My prayers are generally a balance of (A) adoration, (C) confession, (T) thanksgiving, and (S) supplication.

b) My prayers generally default to (S) supplication.

5. Many Christians are prone to downplay the use of the physical body in prayer, since its value in this life is relativized by the unseen and invisible (1 Tim. 4:8). However, what you do with your body often has profound effect on your soul and the state and health of your inner life. Consider the posture of your body and the use of your voice in prayer.

a) Circle the actions that best describe your prayer time: kneel / stand / sit down / lay face down / lay face up / pray silently in my head / pray audibly in a whisper or normal volume / pray in written or typed words

b) Explain what your posture communicates about your prayer.

6. Take a few moments to review what has been said up to this point about "hearing God's voice" in the Bible and "having his ear" in prayer. Outline, summarize, or illustrate below what you would like the general routine of your daily devotions to be like. (My own way of putting it is "begin with Bible reading, move into meditation, polish with prayer.")

Day 15

Pray with Constancy and Company

Pray without ceasing.
1 Thessalonians 5:17

Read chapter 9 (pp. 107–16).

1. "Pray without ceasing" (1 Thess. 5:17); "be constant in prayer" (Rom. 12:12); "pray at all times" (Eph. 6:18). These verses, found in the section "Taking Prayer into the Day," all share the same point. Explain the aim of these verses to the person who says God doesn't intend to keep us on our knees all day long.

2. In the section "Taking Prayer into the Day," I quoted Tim Keller, who writes, "Everywhere God is, prayer is. Since God is everywhere and infinitely great, prayer must be all-pervasive in our lives." Describe or illustrate the times and/or places in the rough and tumble of life that you find yourself sensing the desire to pray.

3. Refer to the section "Christ and His Company."

   a) State what you learned from considering Jesus's habit of praying with others.

   b) Draw a graph, or illustrate in some other way, the importance of corporate prayer in the life of Jesus and his disciples and in the early church.

4. Reflect on your own inclinations in public prayer.

   a) Circle the statement that best describes you:

   - I tend to pray aloud quickly.

   - I am often preoccupied with trying to impress others rather than genuinely speaking to God.

   - I am generally too shy or afraid to pray aloud.

   - I am often worried that I might say something wrong or that others will think that either I am inadequate or my prayer is.

   b) Complete the following statements to make them true:

   - In order to be part of a praying community, I need to . . .

   - God, please help me . . .

5. Refer to the section "Nine Profits of Praying with Company," and identify the ones you most needed to hear. Write them below. Put an asterisk (*) by the profit(s) you intend to pursue right away.

6. Choose and complete the statement below that best describes you:

a) I have ongoing commitments to pray with . . .

b) I do not have ongoing commitments to pray with company, but I plan to initiate regular prayer time with . . .

Day 16

Sharpen Your Affections with Fasting

The disciples of John came to him, saying, "Why do we and the Pharisees fast, but your disciples do not fast?" And Jesus said to them, "Can the wedding guests mourn as long as the bridegroom is with them? The days will come when the bridegroom is taken away from them, and then they will fast."

Matthew 9:14–15

Read chapter 10 (pp. 117–26).

1. Refer to the section "What Is Fasting?"

a) Define fasting.

b) List some "good things," other than food and drink, from which you could consider fasting for some spiritual purpose.

2. Continue to focus on the section "What Is Fasting?" In this section, I said that fasting is a means of God's grace. List some of the gifts God gives through fasting, and put an asterisk (*) beside the most significant, all-encompassing gift.

3. At the beginning of this chapter, I point out the misconceptions that accompany thinking about fasting as merely a duty to perform, instead of focusing on the joy it can bring. Consider your own heart and your experience with fasting. Explain or illustrate many Christians' misunderstanding of it.

4. Consider the placement of fasting here in part 2, with prayer and "having God's ear," rather than in part 1, with God's word and "hearing his voice." Refer to John Piper's quote in the section "Put an Edge on Your Feelings." Answer the following questions:

   a) How does he describe the relationship of fasting to prayer?

   b) Why does he describe fasting as the "handmaiden of prayer"?

5. Eating and drinking, and abstaining, reveal a lot about our hearts. Eating and drinking, though routine and seemingly menial, are not inconsequential but means by which we succeed or fail to glorify God. "Whether you eat or drink, or whatever you do, do all to the glory of God" (1 Cor. 10:31). Fasting (along with feasting, see page 120, note 4) is part of a larger theology of food and drink. Spend a few minutes reflecting on the following three texts. Summarize or illustrate, after each Scripture, what your own eating, drinking, and fasting reveal about the condition of your heart.

- Luke 12:22–23: "Do not be anxious about your life, what you will eat. . . . For life is more than food."

- Luke 12:19–21: The rich man said to his soul, "'Soul, you have ample goods laid up for many years; relax, eat, drink, be merry.' But God said to him, 'Fool! This night your soul is required of you, and the things you have prepared, whose will they be?' So is the one who lays up treasure for himself and is not rich toward God."

- 1 Corinthians 15:32: "If the dead are not raised, 'Let us eat and drink, for tomorrow we die'" (see also Isa. 22:13; 56:12).

6. Reflect on your fasting experience. Describe or illustrate:

a) a time when you undertook a spiritual fast (not just missing a meal).

b) the conditions/motivations that led you to begin fasting.

c) the barriers in your heart that have kept you from fasting.

7. Take a few moments to plan a fast. Illustrate your plan below. Draw a dinner plate, a fork, and a napkin. Add (1) to the rim of the plate a specific spiritual purpose; (2) to the center of the plate a meal, or multiple meals, to miss (be sure to consider how your fasting plans might affect others in your life); (3) on the fork handle a spiritually significant action to fill the time you'd regularly be devoting to eating. Return to this space to reflect on your fasting experience. On the napkin add the take-away you gleaned from your experience.

Journal as a Pathway to Joy

By the grace given to me I say to everyone among you not to think of himself more highly than he ought to think, but to think with sober judgment, each according to the measure of faith that God has assigned.

Romans 12:3

Read chapter 11 (pp. 127–35).

1. Refer to the section "No Wrong Way, No Obligation." Draw two columns below. Title one column "A Journal Is . . ." Title the other column "A Journal Is Not . . ." Add appropriate descriptions to each column.

2. Stay with the section "No Wrong Way, No Obligation." Explain or illustrate what transforms journaling from a common practice into a habit of grace.

3. Scan back over the section "Why Journal?" through the section "To Enrich the Present." (1) List some of the motivations for journaling. (2) Place an asterisk (*) beside items in your list that apply especially to Christians. (3) Circle the motivation that best represents your incentive for journaling.

4. Refer to the subsection "Meditate." Explain or illustrate how journaling can serve as the handmaid of meditation.

5. Describe or illustrate the effect journaling might have on your prayer life.

6. Critics might say that journaling constricts your love for others, because it's an individual and introspective activity that pulls you away from the world to reflect and write. Describe or illustrate how the opposite can be true—that journaling can serve your love for others.

7. If you have any experience journaling, reflect on what you have found most helpful about it. List or illustrate any additional benefits you have thought of.

8. Journaling can be used as a habit of grace for your joy, the good of others, and the glory of God. Make a plan for journaling below.

- Draw four blank journal pages below. Title one page "My Goals," another page "Types of Entries I Plan to Use," and another "My Schedule." Fill in each page with the appropriate information.

- Title the remaining page "My Discovery." Practice journaling for a few days, then return here to describe what you discovered about the habit of journaling.

9. Craft a brief practice journal entry. Write at least one sentence of a prayer or a meditation on truth or a reflection on today's events.

Day 18

Take a Break from the Chaos

Be still, and know that I am God.
Psalm 46:10

Read chapter 12 (pp. 137–42).

1. Refer to the section "Silence and Solitude." Unlike journaling, Jesus himself did practice the habits of silence and solitude. Review Matthew 4:1; 14:23; Mark 1:35; and Luke 4:42. Answer the following:

   a) What spiritual benefit did Jesus derive from purposefully getting away?

   b) How does observing Jesus's retreats affect your perspective on making time for your own retreats?

2. Pay attention to the section "Voices in the Silence." Explain or illustrate how silence and solitude can become habits of grace.

3. Review the section "Beware the Dangers."

a) Draw two columns below. Title the left column "Commonalities." Title the other column "Ways to Go Bad." In the left column list the commonalities that fasting shares with silence and solitude, and in the other column list the ways both habits can go bad.

b) Explain what your chart reveals about:

- the nature of these habits

- the context of these habits

- the limitations of these habits

4. Draw a beach scene. Add a beach umbrella and a boom box or other distracting device (tablet, computer, or smartphone). Title the umbrella "Helpful Practices for Silence and Solitude." Title the device "Unhelpful Practices for Silence and Solitude." Add to the appropriate items helpful and unhelpful practices you have tried in the past.

5. Complete the following statements to make them true.

a) My instinctive response to silence and solitude is . . .

b) This response reveals my desire to/for . . .

c) This response reveals my fears of . . .

d) This response reveals my sins of . . .

e) I need the Spirit's help to grow, heal, and overcome . . .

6. Draw a miniature outline of yourself below. Add a thought bubble. Add words or a picture to the thought bubble that show what you want your "daily respite" (or "quiet time") to look like.

7. Pretend you have 48 hours away, by yourself, at a retreat center nestled in a beautiful outdoor setting; modest meals will be provided three times each day. You will arrive early afternoon on Monday and depart late morning on Wednesday. Draw a page from a personal planner below that includes calendar space for Monday, Tuesday, and Wednesday, and a space marked "Notes." Enter your hourly schedule for these three days in the calendar space. List in the notes space items you would bring to your retreat. (Perhaps look at your real calendar and make plans for an actual retreat.)

Part 3

BELONG TO HIS BODY

Fellowship

Day 19

Learn to Fly in the Fellowship

Take care, brothers, lest there be in any of you an evil, unbelieving heart, leading you to fall away from the living God. But exhort one another every day, as long as it is called "today," that none of you may be hardened by the deceitfulness of sin.

Hebrews 3:12–13

Read chapter 13, from the beginning through the section "Making Fellowship Official" (pp. 145–50).

1. Refer to the introductory paragraphs.

a. Draw two circles so that they partially overlap. Title one circle "New Testament Fellowship." Title the other circle "Modern Church Fellowship." Write the distinctive characteristics of each kind of church fellowship in the appropriate circle. Write the characteristics of fellowship both churches share in the overlapping section.

b. Answer the following questions about your circle diagram.

- What, if anything, did you write in the overlapping section?

- How might the Christian life today be different if the church as a whole thought of fellowship as the New Testament church did?

2. Refer to the section "Partnership for the Gospel." Describe, explain, or illustrate:

a) the relationship between true fellowship and gospel mission.

b) how investing in our relationships with one another in the church helps, rather than hinders, our witness to the world.

3. Read Hebrew 3:12–13 and refer to the section "Be the Means for Your Brother."

a) Explain or illustrate why the instruction of Hebrews 3:12–13 lands not on the weak, struggling brother, but on the community as a whole.

b) Think of those in your church community who are too spiritually weak and fragile right now to fight for their own faith and need the community to actively pursue them and speak truth with grace. Identify some practical ways you can serve as a tangible means of God's grace for them.

4. Shift attention to the section "The Glorious Backstop of Grace."

a) Describe how true Christian fellowship has served as a "backstop" for your faith (or for someone you know) in a season of struggle.

b) Explain what other Christians should provide when your heart is beat down and fragile, and you feel unable to pray and access God's word for yourself.

5. Go to the section "Making Fellowship Official." Explain or illustrate what is needed to transform a "community regular" into a covenant member.

6. Trace your ring finger. Add a wedding band to your finger if you, as a member of a local church, have made formal promises and vows "to be the church" to other members in good times and bad, in sickness and in health. List how being a covenant

member has affected your life. If not a church member, use the space to reflect on what church membership would mean to your life, both in terms of energy invested for others and benefits you would receive.

7. Review the lists of gifts in Romans 12:6–8; 1 Corinthians 12:7–11; and 1 Peter 4:10–11. Keep in mind that none of these are meant to be exhaustive. Consider ways you can be a means of grace to others in the church. Draw a vertical line. On the left side of the line, list your particular giftings. On the other side, list the way each gifting can meet specific needs of those in your church.

Day 20

Lessons in Good Listening

Know this, my beloved brothers: let every person be quick to hear, slow to speak, slow to anger.

James 1:19

In chapter 13 read the section "Six Lessons in Good Listening" to the end of the chapter (pp. 150–54).

1. Rewrite and/or complete the following statements to make them true.

a) I have often thought about intentionally working on the discipline of listening.

b) Before reading this, I heard about the process of becoming a better listener from . . .

c) Some things I have previously learned about becoming a better listener are . . .

2. Describe a time when what you (or someone you know) really needed was for someone to care enough to listen.

3. Draw an earplug and a heart. List the internal attitudes or beliefs that keep your ear plugged. Name or draw the heart treasure these internal earplugs reveal.

4. "The purpose in a man's heart is like deep water, but a man of understanding will draw it out" (Prov. 20:5).

a) Circle the underlined word or phrase that best describes you: I am <u>unskilled</u> / <u>somewhat skilled</u> / <u>skilled</u> / <u>very skilled</u> at asking careful questions to draw others out and perhaps point them to a fresh perspective.

b) Reread the section "Good Listening Asks Perceptive Questions." Be intentional about asking good questions in at least one conversation today. Return to the space below to report your fieldwork.

5. In the section "Good Listening Is Ministry," I quoted Dietrich Bonhoeffer, who said that "listening can be a greater service than speaking."

a) Circle the statement that best describes your reaction to Bonhoefffer's words.

- I'm surprised; the quote doesn't seem to be true.

- I see the truth in the quote.

b) Give an example, real or imagined, when listening was a greater service to a friend or family member, believer or unbeliever, than speaking.

6. Bonhoeffer said, "Anyone who thinks that his time is too valuable to spend keeping quiet [by listening] will eventually have no time for God and his brother, but only for himself and for his own follies." (See the section "Good Listening Reflects Our Relationship with God.")

a) Circle the statement (or add a statement) that best describes your reaction to someone who really needs you to listen:

- My face reveals stress, and I think, "Hurry up! I'm extremely busy."

- I roll my eyes, tap my fingers, look at the time, and think, "Why me?"

- Other:

b) Explain or illustrate how good listening reflects your relationship with God.

c) Write out a short prayer below, asking God for his mercy. Ask him to make you a better listener by first and foremost tuning your heart to listen more carefully to his words of life and grace.

7. Conclude today's study by reading Janet Dunn's article "How to Become a Good Listener" (available at www.desiringGod.org/articles/how-to-become-a-good-listener). List any notes or fresh resolves below.

Day 21

Kindle the Fire in Corporate Worship

Whom have I in heaven but you?
   And there is nothing on earth that I desire besides you.
My flesh and my heart may fail,
   but God is the strength of my heart and my portion forever.

Psalm 73:25–26

Read chapter 14 from the beginning through the section "The Secret of Joy: Self-Forgetfulness" (pp. 155–59).

1. Complete the statement that best represents your reaction to the claim that corporate worship is the single most important means of God's grace.

- I agree because . . .

- I disagree because . . .

2. Review the sections "The Most Important Means of Grace," "Worship Is No Means," and "The Secret of Joy: Self-Forgetfulness."

a) Explain the problem of saying that corporate worship is a means of grace while also saying worship is not a means to anything.

b) Explain or illustrate how to resolve this problem.

3. Describe "the secret of worship" (see the section "The Secret of Joy: Self-Forgetfulness") and how this secret should affect your perspective when gathering this weekend, and every weekend, in corporate worship.

4. The corporate worship gathering of your church may or may not be manifestly preoccupied with Jesus. Regardless of whether it is or isn't, there are things you can do to prepare your mind and heart for worship. Describe or illustrate what you can do the night before and/or the morning of corporate worship to be ready for this means of grace.

5. In the following lesson we will consider some of the benefits of corporate worship. Before you get there, consider now, both from what you've read as well as from your experience, some of the benefits of worshiping Jesus together. List the benefits you thought of here.

6. Imagine a friend has expressed to you his disillusionment with corporate worship. He was beginning to think he didn't really need to be "in church" each weekend. He argued that it would be more beneficial just to listen to sermons online and have friendships with fellow Christians throughout the week. Use the space below to make the case for the importance of corporate worship in the Christian life.

Day 22

The Benefits of Corporate Worship

For me it is good to be near God;
I have made the Lord GOD my refuge,
that I may tell of all your works.

Psalm 73:28

In chapter 14 read the section "Five Benefits of Corporate Worship" through the end of the chapter (pp. 159–63).

1. Draw a church and a heart below. Inside the church, list one or two of the five benefits of corporate worship (found in chapter 14) that appeal to you most. Inside the heart, write what your choice reveals about your heart's attitude. Draw an arrow to show the relationship between the church and your heart.

2. Describe or illustrate:

   a) a time you were spiritually lethargic and tempted to stay away from corporate worship.

   b) a time you experienced an awakening from some spiritual sluggishness or indifference in corporate worship.

c) what truth(s) your heart needs to hear when you are spiritually lethargic and tempted to stay away from worship.

3. Explain or illustrate how corporate worship strengthens your assurance that you are truly born again. (Refer to the subsection "Assurance.")

4. Review the subsection "Accentuated Joy."

a) Describe or illustrate the richness and depth of joy you have felt in corporate worship.

b) Write a statement or draw a picture that describes the difference between the joy you have felt in corporate worship and the joy you have felt in private worship.

5. List any additional benefits of corporate worship you can think of. Then compare this list to the one you made in the previous lesson (see question 5 in lesson 21). Explain how the lists are different.

Listen for Grace in the Pulpit

Preach the word; be ready in season and out of season; reprove, rebuke, and exhort, with complete patience and teaching.

2 Timothy 4:2

Read chapter 15 (pp. 165–71).

1. Preaching has fallen on hard times in some circles. Draw two stick figures. Add a voice bubble to one figure and a thought bubble to the other. In the voice bubble write negative things you have heard people say about the act of preaching. In the thought bubble write negative things you have thought about the act of preaching.

2. Scan the chapter again. Notice the emphasis placed on encountering Jesus through the preached word. Draw another stick figure to represent yourself. Add a voice bubble. Use points from this chapter to write your response to the two stick figures above.

3. Go back to the introductory paragraphs of this chapter. Locate the phrase "the climactic grace." Explain or illustrate why preaching, of the many elements of corporate worship, is "the climactic grace."

4. Refer to the subsection "Experience the Joy." Identify "the great goal of preaching." Draw a football and a football goal below. On the football identify the great goal of preaching. To the football goal add your description of how to attain this great goal.

5. List some of the five benefits of faithful preaching that are especially persuasive to you. Perhaps you've experienced other benefits. Add those to your list.

Day 24

Wash in the Waters Again

Do you not know that all of us who have been baptized into Christ Jesus were baptized into his death? We were buried therefore with him by baptism into death, in order that, just as Christ was raised from the dead by the glory of the Father, we too might walk in newness of life.

Romans 6:3–4

Read chapter 16 (pp. 173–77).

1. Refer to the introductory paragraphs. Explain:

a) the phrase "visible words."

b) how baptism and the Lord's Supper are "visible words" for the church.

c) how the "visible words" of baptism and the Lord's Supper engage your five senses.

2. Perhaps you remember your baptism. If so, describe or illustrate the details you remember.

3. Refer to the section "The Sacraments as Means of Grace." Circle the answer that best completes this statement: The ordinances, including baptism, "renew and strengthen our sense of being united by faith to the risen Christ . . .

  a) apart from faith.

  b) through the power of the Holy Spirit by faith.

  c) without faith.

4. Baptism, along with church membership, is one means of affirming your faith. By your baptism, a trustworthy body of believers affirms that your confession of faith in Jesus is credible. This affirmation is beneficial when you are battling temptation, doubt, or weakness. Describe some memorable moments (baptism or something else) in your life that have provided affirmation and helped you do battle.

5. Refer to the section "Improve Your Baptism." Explain, describe, or illustrate:

  a) the term "improving our baptism."

b) a time you experienced "improvement" through watching with faith the baptism of someone else.

6. Imagine that a friend has come to faith in Christ but is delaying baptism. Draw two stick figures to represent you and your friend. Add a voice bubble to yourself. In the voice bubble, add reasons you would give your friend (other than raw obedience to Christ's command) for pursuing baptism.

Day 25

Grow in Grace at the Table

I received from the Lord what I also delivered to you, that the Lord Jesus on the night when he was betrayed took bread, and when he had given thanks, he broke it, and said, "This is my body which is for you. Do this in remembrance of me." In the same way also he took the cup, after supper, saying, "This cup is the new covenant in my blood. Do this, as often as you drink it, in remembrance of me." For as often as you eat this bread and drink the cup, you proclaim the Lord's death until he comes.

1 Corinthians 11:23–26

Read chapter 17 (pp. 179–83).

1. Refer to the introductory paragraphs of chapter 17. Circle the statement that best completes this sentence: The key principles behind the means of grace are . . .

a) Jesus's voice (word), Jesus's ear (prayer), and Jesus's body (church).

b) Read the Bible, pray, attend church, and check the boxes.

c) Do nothing and wait on God's grace to meet you where you are.

2. In the introductory paragraphs, I claimed that few, if any, other practices bring together all three principles of grace like the preaching of God's word and the celebration of the sacraments in the context of corporate worship. Draw a dinner table. Place a microphone, an ear, and some stick figures on the table. Explain how the

graces of "hearing the Lord's voice," "having his ear," and "belonging to the Lord's body" converge at the Lord's Table.

3. Refer to the section "The Gravity: Blessing or Judgment." Explain or illustrate:

  a) "the gravity" of the Table.

  b) why it is so important not to handle the elements lightly and partake "in an unworthy manner"?

  c) the blessing for those who eat in faith.

d) the curse for those who eat without faith.

4. Refer to the section "The Present: Proclaiming His Death." Consider the corporate dynamic at work in celebrating the Lord's Supper. When we partake, we "proclaim the Lord's death until he comes" (1 Cor. 11:26). Explain or illustrate how (1) your participation feeds and strengthens your own soul by faith, and (2) your participation serves to strengthen and encourage others.

5. Since the Reformation in the sixteenth century, the Christian church has been deeply divided over the theology and practice of the Lord's Supper. The Catholic Church believes the bread and wine, though maintaining the physical properties of bread and wine, become in essence the body and blood of Christ; they are "transubstantiated," meaning the "substance" or reality of the bread and wine are changed, while the "accidents" (what are accessible to our senses) remain unchanged. In response, many low-church traditions tend to emphasize what is *not* happening at the Table as much as what is—and what *is* happening is merely a memorial, and no more. The Reformed tradition, which is essentially the perspective of this chapter, sees the Table as a means of grace by which our souls are nourished and strengthened as we partake in faith.

a. Describe your church's theology and practice of the Lord's Supper.

b. Explain why you do (or why you do not) find the Reformed perspective of the Lord's Supper, along with its accompanying Scripture quotations, compelling.

6. One question that often arises in regard to the Lord's Supper is whether the Supper may be shared outside of the context of corporate worship in the life of a local church—for instance, at a youth retreat, at a family dinner, or for the bride and groom at a wedding. Read 1 Corinthians 11 again and reflect on what you learned in chapter 17. Write or illustrate below your answer to the question: Is it appropriate to share the Supper at a private gathering?

7. Focus on 1 Corinthians 11:17–34 and explain, in context:

a) what it means to partake of the Supper "in an unworthy manner" (v. 27).

b) what it means to eat and drink "without discerning the body" (v. 29).

c) two possible meanings of the term "body of Christ" in this context.

Day 26

Embrace the Blessing of Rebuke

Let a righteous man strike me—it is a kindness;
    let him rebuke me—it is oil for my head;
    let my head not refuse it.

Psalm 141:5

Read chapter 18 through the section "Unlock the Power" (pp. 185–89).

1. Perhaps there was a time when a friend spoke truth into your life and, though it stung at first, you soon realized the truth was for your good. Describe or illustrate that time.

2. Maybe you have been on the receiving end of correction and have learned from experience what to do (and what not to do) when giving correction. Imagine the situation is reversed and now you must give correction. Draw a vertical line below. List on the left side of the line what you would like to do when giving correction. List on the right side of the line what you've learned not to do.

3. Review the sections "Watershed of Wisdom" and "Open the Gift."

a) Circle the responses that best describe your reactions when you hear corrective words from a person who genuinely loves you.

- I am embarrassed.
- I bristle in anger.
- I experience fear.
- I receive corrective words of rebuke as an act of love.
- Other:

b) Rewrite or complete the following statement to make it true:

When I don't receive correction as a gift, it is because . . .

4. Take a few moments to examine yourself. Complete the following:

a) The sinful (thought, attitude, action) patterns that I am aware of in my life right now are . . .

b) My current indwelling sin is manifested when . . .

c) Right now I need to hear the following words of rebuke:

d) Right now I need to hear the following corrective words:

Day 27

Give the Blessing of Rebuke

Brothers, if anyone is caught in any transgression, you who are spiritual should restore him in a spirit of gentleness. Keep watch on yourself, lest you too be tempted.

Galatians 6:1

In chapter 18 read from the section "Give the Blessing of Rebuke" to the end of the chapter (pp. 189–94).

1. In the first few paragraphs in the section "Give the Blessing of Rebuke," I said that one of the most loving things we can do for someone is tell them when they're in the wrong. Write your response to that statement.

2. Review the subsection "Seek to Sympathize." Explain or illustrate:

   a) the term "the Golden Rule of Rebuke."

b) how keeping the Golden Rule of Rebuke in mind motivates you to graciously initiate a rebuke or correction toward a brother or sister in Christ when you observe some misdeed or sinful tendency.

3. Carefully read Matthew 18:15–17; Hebrews 3:12–13; Luke 17:3–4; 2 Thessalonians 3:14–15; and James 5:19–20. Record your observations related to giving the blessing of rebuke in loving humility. Note in particular how each text makes restoration the aim of correction.

4. Perhaps you have experienced that awkward moment as you offer a word of correction to someone. Or maybe you have experienced the inner turmoil of needing to provide a word of correction, but something kept you from it. Identify and describe a particular experience. Include why you chose to correct or why you didn't.

5. Describe or illustrate the lessons you have learned if you have provided correction for others.

6. Your personality and particular wiring affect whether confrontation is easy or difficult for you. And all of us are conditioned by our society, which for most of us makes us less likely to embrace the awkward moment of rebuke. Explain how your personality and society's influence affect your willingness to give correction to a Christian brother or sister.

7. Scan back over the seven steps in the section "Give the Blessing of Rebuke."

a) Draw a horizontal line below. Write "Easy" on one end of the line and "Difficult" on the other. Add some points along the line. Choose a few of the seven steps and label the points along your line with these steps to show which are easier and which are harder for you.

b) Explain how this information will affect the way you will pray when you realize the need to rebuke a fellow Christian.

8. In light of James 5:19–20, consider your own life and the lives of those in Christ around you. Perhaps there was a time in your life when you were wandering, and someone, serving as a God-appointed means of grace to bring you back, spoke words of rebuke to you. Identify those in your life right now who are wandering. Consider whether God may be calling you to lovingly and humbly speak a kind, clear word of rebuke. Write your prayer for restoration below. (Refer to step 3 if you need help with this prayer.)

Part 4

CODA

The Commission: Disciple the Nations

What you have heard from me in the presence of many witnesses entrust to faithful men who will be able to teach others also.

2 Timothy 2:2

Being affectionately desirous of you, we were ready to share with you not only the gospel of God but also our own selves, because you had become very dear to us.

1 Thessalonians 2:8

Read chapter 19 (pp. 197–203).

1. Refer to the introductory paragraphs. Draw two circles below. Draw a clock and a dollar inside one circle. Title this circle "The Great Commission." Draw a Bible, praying hands, and a church in the other circle. Title this circle "Habits of Grace." Use words, arrows, lines, or whatever you choose to show the relationship between the two circles.

2. Refer to the section "Disciplemaking as a Means of Grace."

   a) Define *disciplemaking*.

   b) Describe your experience with disciplemaking, either as a discipler or as a disciple or both.

3. In the beginning paragraphs of the section "Disciplemaking as a Means of Grace," I said that good disciplemaking is always a two-way street. Describe a time when you have seen or experienced this truth.

4. Explain or illustrate how the simple, unglamorous practice of disciplemaking connects the bigness of God's global purposes with the smallness of our everyday lives.

5. Disciplemaking requires both intentionality and "relationality."

   a) Draw an upside-down triangle below. Title the triangle "My Inclinations and Tendencies." Draw an off-centered vertical line through the triangle. Title one space in the triangle "Naturally Relational" and title the remaining space

"Intentional" so that the largest area of the triangle represents your strongest inclination, your natural leaning.

b) Explain what you need to do to balance these tendencies.

6. Identify one good thing that you, as a sinner, can model in disciplemaking that Jesus, who was not a sinner, did not. Explain the importance of modeling this early and often in a discipling relationship.

7. Good disciplers must learn how to deal well with failure. Explain (1) why, and (2) what spiritual benefit that dealing with failure brings to the Christian life.

8. The prospect of disciplemaking often stirs up fear. Internal barriers may keep you from sharing your words and your life with those who need salvation or growth in Christlikeness.

a) List the fears (internal barriers) that keep you from initiating disciple-making.

b) Write a prayer that addresses the need to overcome these fears.

9. Good disciplemaking begins with prayer. Identify at least one person, but not more than three, who are already in your life (whether believers or unbelievers) that may benefit spiritually from regular, intentional time with you. Begin praying that God would provide (1) informal opportunities, at first, for you to build the relationship and, in due course, (2) more regular, formal, focused meetings to pursue health and growth in Jesus. Write out your prayer below.

Day 29

The Dollar: Test Your True Treasure

You know the grace of our Lord Jesus Christ, that though he was rich, yet for your sake he became poor, so that you by his poverty might become rich. . . . Each one must give as he has decided in his heart, not reluctantly or under compulsion, for God loves a cheerful giver.

2 Corinthians 8:9; 9:7

Read chapter 20 (pp. 205–10).

1. Generosity is one of the great evidences that one is truly a Christian. Explain or illustrate:

a) why this is so.

b) what your generosity clearly communicates about the gospel.

2. The *love* of money causes so many problems that it can be easy to think the problem is money itself. However, the problem is not external to us; it's in us. The trouble is not money itself but our hearts. Describe or illustrate how money can be good for the Great Commission and the advance of God's kingdom.

3. Review Matthew 17:27; 22:21; and Luke 16:9. Summarize or illustrate Jesus's view of money.

4. Draw two hearts below. Title one heart "Hoarding Heart." Title the other heart "Giving Heart." Draw or name the treasure that is kept inside each heart.

5. Refer to the section "Sacrifice Varies from Person to Person."

a) Draw a horizontal line below. Title the line "My Sacrifice." Add two points on each end and two points between. Label the points from left to right "Never," "Sometimes," "Often," and "Always." Draw an "X" on the line to show the degree to which you abstain from "the needs of this life" in order to give to others.

b) Describe ways that you already sacrifice in order to give *or* describe ways you plan to sacrifice in order to give.

6. Scan the section "Generosity Is a Means of Grace." Draw a cross. Title the upper left space "Evidences of Generosity in My Life." Title the upper right space "Evidences of Selfishness in My Life." Title the lower left space "Reasons I Should Grow in Generosity." Title the lower right space "Ways I Plan to Grow in Generosity." Fill in each space with the appropriate information.

Day 30

The Clock: Manage Your Time
in the Mission of Love

Look carefully then how you walk, not as unwise but as wise, making the best use of the time, because the days are evil. Therefore do not be foolish, but understand what the will of the Lord is.

Ephesians 5:15–17

Read chapter 21 (pp. 211–18).

1. Refer to the introductory paragraphs of the chapter and to the first section, "If the Lord Wills."

a) Name the two sinful extremes related to time management.

b) Describe examples in your life of either, or both, extremes.

2. Perhaps you have felt the allure of "productivity porn," described in the section with that name.

a) Draw a vertical line. On one side of the line, list the ways you want to and have tried to increase efficiency and effectiveness in the use of your time. On the other side of the line, list the actual improvements and growth in productivity you've experienced.

b. Name the motivation that drives the desires you listed.

3. Refer to the section "Faith Working through Love." Explain or illustrate how time management becomes truly Christian.

4. Circle the statement(s) that best describes the current state of your time management:

a) Most days time just slips away, and I don't really know what I did with it.

b) By the time I finish with my job, my kids, my spouse, and the house, there is no time left to manage.

c) I intend to be more productive, but then my spouse wants to watch a show or movie, or my friend wants to visit over coffee, or my church needs a volunteer, so I usually opt for those more enjoyable activities.

d) I am scrupulous with my time. I try to never waste a minute, no matter what.

e) My schedule is motivated by my love for others, and I stick to it.

f) Other:

5. Consider the calling(s) operative in your life right now. Draw four circles that partially overlap. Title one circle "Desires," one "Giftings," one "Affirmation of Others," and the remaining circle "God's Providential Opportunity." List desires, giftings, affirmations, and opportunities in the appropriate circles. Identify the desire that matches with a gifting affirmed by others that you have an opportunity to use right now. Write that information in the overlapping area.

6. In the subsection "Make the Most of Your Mornings," I said that where your morning is, there your heart will be also. Draw a miniature outline of yourself below. Put the first thing(s) you run to each morning in your hand(s). Add a heart. Look at the thing(s) in your hand(s). Determine what heart treasure they reveal. Draw that treasure inside your heart.

7. Look back over the subsection "Create Flexibility for Meeting Others' Needs."

   a) Explain or illustrate what it means to proactively guard your time.

   b) Explain or illustrate what it means to reactively give your time.

   c) Draw two analog clocks below—the kind with the numbers and the hands that move. Title one "Morning" and the other "Evening." Add to your clocks the numbers 1 to 12. Add notes around the clocks to show how you plan to adjust your day so that you can proactively guard and reactively give your time to others.

Day 31

Communing with Christ on a Crazy Day

[Jesus] said to me, "My grace is sufficient for you, for my power is made perfect in weakness." Therefore I will boast all the more gladly of my weaknesses, so that the power of Christ may rest upon me.

2 Corinthians 12:9

Read the epilogue (pp. 219–23).

1. Describe or illustrate the opportunity that is presented when your morning routine is interrupted, and you suddenly sense yourself to be spiritually weak.

2. I mentioned earlier that my summary for the morning routine I've developed over the years is "begin with Bible reading, move to meditation, polish with prayer." With a flexible routine like this, I can easily add time for longer meditation and prayer and also make time for memorization and journaling on more leisurely mornings. Record the sequence of your morning routine. Add the minutes you ideally would devote to each element. Circle elements that can be abbreviated so that you can still have a channel of spiritual refreshment on a crazy day.

3. Describe the value of fellowship as a means of grace on a crazy day.

4. Think back to your last "crazy day"; perhaps it is even today. Answer the following questions:

a) What made it crazy—something the night before or something unplanned the morning of, or both?

b) What lesson, if any, can you learn from this instance that might help you avoid some of the craziness and better prepare you to commune with Christ?

5. Imagine some circumstance has constricted your morning, and you have ten minutes to commune with Christ in his word and prayer.

a) Explain how you would apportion those ten minutes between hearing God's voice in the Scriptures and having his ear in prayer.

b) Explain how you would approach your morning "time with God" if you had only two minutes.

6. Looking back now on the entirety of this study, what three things seem most important to take away and apply to your life?

7. How do you hope the trajectory of your life will be different because of this study? Capture it below in the form of a written prayer to God.

About the Author

David Mathis (@davidcmathis) is executive editor of desiringGod.org and has served as editor and publications manager for pastor and author John Piper since 2006. He is a pastor for Cities Church in Minneapolis, Minnesota, and an adjunct professor at Bethlehem College & Seminary.

David grew up in Spartanburg, South Carolina, and graduated from Furman University in Greenville, South Carolina. He came to Minneapolis to study at The Bethlehem Institute (now Bethlehem College & Seminary) and minister on the college campus with Campus Outreach. David is married to Megan, and they have twin sons and a daughter.

David first taught spiritual disciplines to college students while on staff with Campus Outreach and now teaches "habits of grace" to college students at Bethlehem College & Seminary. He has written about the means of grace at desiringGod.org and continues to write there regularly.

desiringGod

Everyone wants to be happy. Our website was born and built for happiness. We want people everywhere to understand and embrace the truth that *God is most glorified in us when we are most satisfied in him*. We've collected more than thirty years of John Piper's speaking and writing, including translations into more than forty languages. We also provide a daily stream of new written, audio, and video resources to help you find truth, purpose, and satisfaction that never end. And it's all available free of charge, thanks to the generosity of people who've been blessed by the ministry.

If you want more resources for true happiness, or if you want to learn more about our work at Desiring God, we invite you to visit us at www.desiringGod.org.

www.desiringGod.org

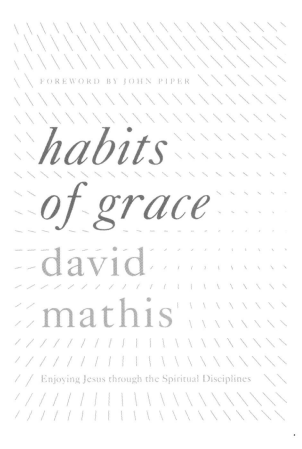

FOREWORD BY JOHN PIPER

habits of grace

david mathis

Enjoying Jesus through the Spiritual Disciplines

978-1-4335-5047-8
Hardcover, $14.99
Available February 2016

ORDERING INFORMATION

ORDER BY PHONE > 800.323.3890

ORDER BY FAX > 630.682.4785

ORDER BY MAIL > 1300 Crescent Street, Wheaton, IL 60187

ORDER BY E-MAIL > sales@crossway.org

ORDER ONLINE > www.crossway.org

FOR CUSTOMER SERVICE, CALL > 800.543.1659